Part One

Thinking and Talking about Learning

How do we think and talk about learning?

In this section you will:

- Build an understanding of the words we use to talk about learning in a helpful way
- See the importance of talk in your learning
- Think about your own learning, your dreams and goals and your responsibilities as a learner

Although we now have so many different ways of communicating with each other, it is important to remember that high quality talk is one of the most important skills we need to develop.

Think about when you use talk:

at school ***with your friends***

at home ***with your family***

Think about when you communicate in other ways... text, social networking, twitter, email etc.

You probably think that you are working best when you are quiet! This is probably because you hear teachers asking you for quiet far more often than they ask you to talk about your learning.

Think about what sort of talk it is that teachers want less of?

Would this be talk that is helpful or unhelpful to learning?

So what is helpful talk?

What is unhelpful talk?

Unhelpful talk
Arguing
Back chat
Interrupting
Gossiping
Teasing
Swearing
Talking when someone else is talking

Helpful Talk
Sharing ideas
Asking questions
Being polite
Encouraging others
Making suggestions
Explaining
Giving instructions

What difference does learning about 'helpful talk' make to learners?

These are the sorts of comments that learners like you have made.

You can make your friends feel better.

It's when you talk about work during work during work time and you are being polite and respectful.

When you compliment someone and make them feel good.

I don't get distracted so easily any more.

You can ask somebody politely if they need help in their work or if they can help you.

We have learned to listen more carefully to what other people have to say and we concentrate much better now which means we can improve our work.

Helping someone if they are stuck and are not sure what to do.

Why do you think talking about learning is important?

To be strong and successful learners, we need to think about what we are actually doing in our learning and be able to talk about it using powerful learning words.

Here is a list of some powerful learning words to get you started:

To get you started…

Achieve

Aim high, aspire

Ask good questions

Be determined

Be enthusiastic

Choose a positive attitude

Deal with disappointments

Develop new skills

Encourage

Focus

Learn from mistakes

Listen

Make an effort

Make choices

Make good choices

Organise

Persevere

Plan

Practice

Problem solve

Reason

Recognise problems

Share ideas with others

Solve problems

Struggle

Support

Think

Understand

Work hard

Add your own powerful learning words here …

Getting to the 'I get it' place.

How many of these words do you know already? What do you think they mean? Can you explain what they mean to someone else?

Use some of the powerful learning words from the list to share your thinking:

What do you do when you don't know what to do?
Think of a real example of when this happened.
How do you stay on task when your learning gets really tough?
Think of a real example of when this happened.

Why do you think we are asking you to do this?
What choices have you made in your learning?

When did you last support someone?

What do you think you need to practice most?

When did you last feel successful?

How do you see yourself as a learner?

What do you feel you are good at? Why?

What do you enjoy learning most? Why?

What does this tell you about yourself?

Use this page in any way you like to show what you are like as a learner. You could draw a picture, make a list, a mind map... anything you like!

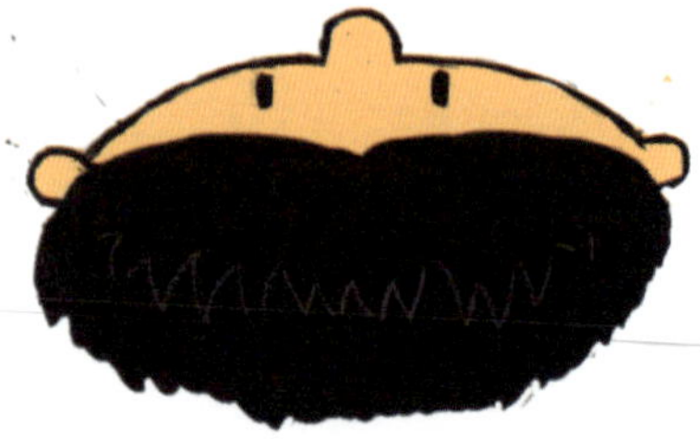

Thinking about goals and dreams...

Think about what you most wish to achieve in ten years from now...

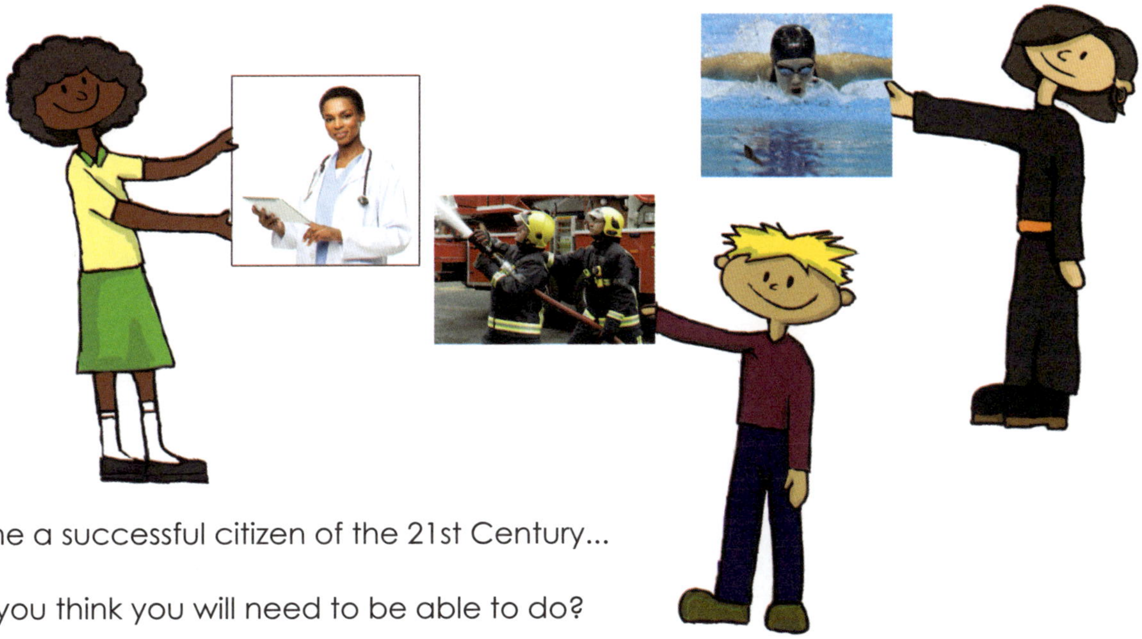

To become a successful citizen of the 21st Century...

What do you think you will need to be able to do?

What do you think you will need to be like?

If today is the beginning of that journey what do you think you need to do from today?

What do you need to be like as a person?

What do you need to do?	What do you need to be like?

My Ambition

I want to be

Why?

What do I have to learn?

Part Two

Bouncebackability

What is 'bouncebackability' and how do you get it?

In this section you will:

- Think about how you feel about your learning and what you can do about it
- Explore what happens when you:
  - *get things wrong*
  - *are disappointed*
  - *don't get your own way*
- Learn about the challenge zone and what it means to be a purple learner!

Turning your brain on and making it work better

You can alter your brain structure easily. The more you learn the more information your brain takes on. Remember you don't just learn at school!

Think about where you learn outside the classroom...

Thinking positive thoughts is very good for your brain no matter where you are

- I can do this… if I…
- I expect to do well in this test because…
- If I really put my mind to it I can…
- I am going to be learning about... What is my challenge?
- What will I do first, and second and then third?
- What might it look like once I have completed it?

When you expect to do well your brain thinks it can. When you think you won't do well, your brain thinks it can't. When you really want to do something, your brain works really well. When you are curious and wondering about something your brain becomes very active.

Keep reminding yourself why you need to do your best.

Keep reminding yourself how you will feel when you do your best.

Thinking about the 'Movers' and 'Blockers' of learning

Think about what **moves** your learning forward and what **blocks** your learning.

Movers: What helps you to learn best?
Blockers: What stops you from learning?

Make a list of your own Movers and Blockers

Movers: what helps you to learn?	Blockers: what stops you from learning?

It is important to build upon the Movers and reduce or remove the Blockers so that we become more powerful learners. So what can **YOU** do about it for yourself?

How does your learning make you feel?

Once we understand how we feel about learning... what can we do about it?

Learning zones: recognising and understanding how we feel about our different learning experiences.

Do we learn more by getting things right or getting things wrong?

Do you think you are a better learner if you try really hard or if you get your work finished?

What could you do when you don't know what to do (except asking the teacher)?

When something in life goes badly and you feel disappointed or angry...
What could you do?

How do we feel when our learning is easy?

If our learning is easy what could/should we do?

How do we feel when our learning is a bit tricky?

If our learning is a bit tricky what could/should we do?

How do we feel when our learning is too hard?

If our learning is too hard what could/should we do about it?

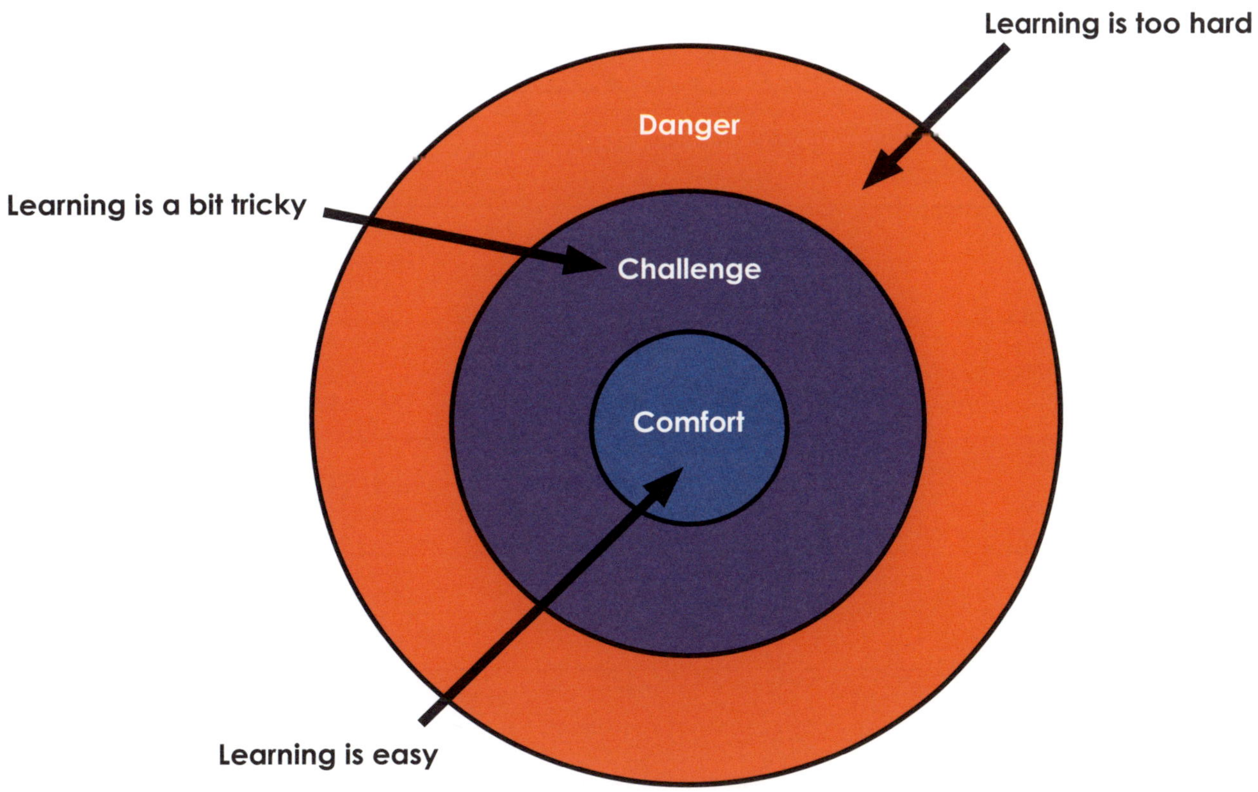

The Danger Zone

Red for danger... **blue** for comfort... **red** and **blue** make...?

So what is a **purple** learner?

Are you a **purple** learner?

What does a **purple** learner do?

Purple learners:
I will be a **purple** learner when I...

try hard
have a go at tricky things
think for myself
make an effort
keep going
do the best that I can!

What else can you think of that **purple** learners do...?

When our learning is easy we are in the Comfort Zone. This can make us feel good because we can celebrate what we have done well and enjoy being able to do more and feel more confident. However we need to understand that we shouldn't just stay there! If we get used to things being easy and straightforward we will become less willing to have a go at more difficult problems and challenges.

To step from our Comfort Zone to our Challenge Zone means we have to be brave. This is when we do things that might make us feel a little anxious and yet we still need to give it a go. The more we allow ourselves to be challenged, the braver we get so we can take on even bigger challenges. Being brave makes us even more successful in life.

However, if we find that our learning is much too challenging we may become fearful and worried and lose confidence in ourselves. If this is the case, we are in the Danger Zone and this can be damaging to us as learners.

When do you decide it's too challenging?

What might you do about it?

When our learning is tricky, we feel challenged and we know that we have to make an effort. We are growing the parts of our brains that help us learn better. This is the place to be for our best learning experiences – this is the Challenge Zone and it is here where we take risks, have a go and try things out.

Are you challenging yourself?

When we are finding our learning really difficult, we may become anxious or worried. We might feel that we just can't do it and perhaps that we are not good enough or clever enough. With the right support, attitude and plenty of effort, we will in time find that it becomes easier and we can do a little... then a little bit more until we feel that perhaps we can do it! We then feel more confident and this can mean that we have more energy to try even harder! Eventually we may find that this piece of learning, which once seemed so difficult and out of reach, is something we can do! This happens to all of us all the time!

Think about how your learning makes you feel in different subjects...

English

Maths

PE

Science

Art

Music

Foreign languages

Dance

Geography

History

Other subjects

... and how learning makes you feel when you learn in different ways.

On your own

With a partner

In a small group

In a larger group

Part 3

Team Learning

How can we make sure that our team learning is high quality?

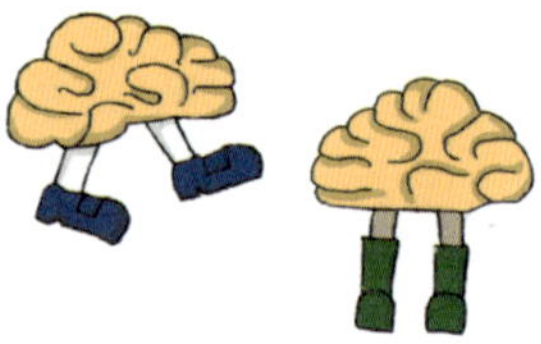

In this section you will:

- Find out what high quality team learning is all about
- Explore the learning gems and how to develop them

Having one brain to help us learn and think is great but having a team of brains to help grow our thinking and learning is sometimes even better.

What will working well together look like and sound like?

Add your ideas to the ones in the boxes:

What will you see?	What will you hear?
People looking at each other Nodding Taking turns	Sharing ideas Questions

What do we have to do to make our team work sparkle?

We all have some very special abilities. These help us learn more about the world in which we live. Each ability is so special we call it after the name of a precious gem. To work as a team you must use all your gem abilities together.

To work as a team you have to use your:

- **Ruby** – being aware of others and how what you do or say, might make them feel

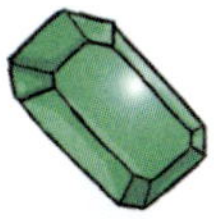

- **Emerald** – bouncing back from mistakes and disappointment, and controlling your anger if it tries to get out!

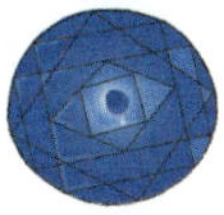

- **Sapphire** – keeping focused and staying in control of the monster distractions

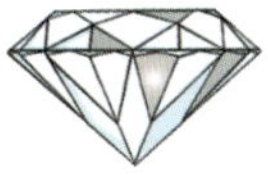

- **Diamond** – being able to notice a problem and thinking of ways to solve it

How much of each of these powers do you have?

Think about:

- Which of the four team work powers do you think you have developed well?
- Which of the four abilities do you think you might need to improve on?
- Why do you think that?

When these powers combine!
To work well with a partner or in larger teams we need to use all the four powers together.

Ruby – for helping us support others and being aware of what they do well
Emerald – for being able to cope with not getting your own way or being disappointed
Sapphire – for keeping focused on what is important
Diamond – for being able to see the problem and work to solve it

- **Amethyst** – cooperation... learning with a partner – applies all the gem powers to work with a partner

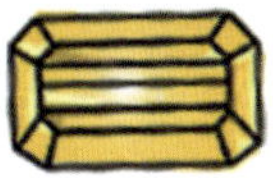

- **Topaz** – collaboration... learning in a big group – applies all the gem powers to work with a team

When you use all these powers with one other person you are getting better at using the Amethyst Power.

When you use all these powers in a team of three or more you are getting better at using the Topaz Power.

High quality group work - Topaz Power

Look at the sentences on the right and think about which box you would put them in. When you put each sentence in the box below, you need to have a reason for putting each of them there.

When we are learning in a group we find it helpful when… because…

When we are learning in a group we find it unhelpful when… because…

We are not sure about these yet... because…

One person does all the talking and no one else feels they can join in.

Every so often, someone in the group sums up where the group has got to, they pull together the main ideas so everyone can decide what to do next.

If you tell everyone your idea other people in your group ask you questions about it to help your idea grow.

Everyone in the group gets a chance to share their ideas.

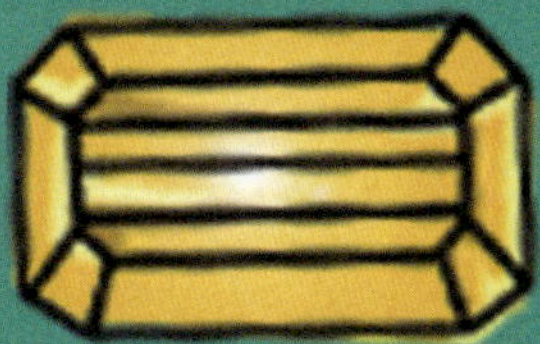

Some people only listen to their friends.

People in your group ask you what you think.

Somebody in the group interrupts you while you are talking.

Some people in your group don't speak or contribute ideas of their own.

If you ask anyone in the group, they all know and understand what they have to do.

Look at the sentences on the right and think about which box you would put them in. When you put each sentence in the box below, you need to have a reason for putting each of them there.

I'm not sure what to do.

I don't have everything I need to get on with my learning.

I don't know where to start.

I'm stuck... I'm not sure what to do next.

Break the work up into little bits and do them one at a time.

Pretend I know what to do and do something.

Read through what I have done to see if it helps.

Check what I need before I start and make sure it's there.

Ask the teacher for a starter sentence.

Borrow from a friend.

Look back at my earlier work to see if that helps.

Work out what has to be done first and do it.

Do what I think, even if it isn't right, and then go back and go over it again. Make changes.

Read the task again to make sure I'm clear about it all.

Go and get what I need from the classroom or the library.

Ask the teacher.

Ask my friend.

Make a start but work very slowly to look as though I am busy.

Copy from the person next to me.

Pretend I know what to do and do nothing.

Developing some team work rules

Think about the sentences below: Tick the box on the right to show what it is that you do now, what you do sometimes or what you definitely need to practice.

When I work in a group I ...
Listen carefully to others in the group
Share my ideas with the rest of the group
Do some of the talking
Encourage others to get agreement
Act as chairperson
Sum up what we have decided
Don't interrupt other people when they are talking
Make sure I understand exactly what the group needs to do
Change my mind if people give good reasons for their opinions
Get upset if people disagree with me
Other suggestions:

What I do now	What I do sometimes	What I definitely need to practice

When I work in a group I ask other people to...
Explain things again that I don't understand
Tell me what they think
Keep to the point
Answer questions about what they've just said
Give reasons for their opinions
Join in if they have not said anything
Say if they don't agree with what I am saying and not worry about it
Other suggestions:

Use your thinking from the previous pages to help you come up with a set of team work rules that everyone in your team must follow:

What I do now	What I do sometimes	What I definitely need to practice

Are there some ideas that you all need to practice before you make them a rule?
What are they?

Display your team work rules in your classroom and put a reminder up about which ones you are all trying to get better at.

These are the rules you need to follow to make sure you get high quality team work:

Part Four

Making Choices

How does making choices help us to become more responsible for our own learning?

In this section you will:

- Understand what being responsible really means
- Think about the choices you make and how you might make changes
- Find out what the Diamond Power does and how you can make more
- Be able to set up the Diamond Power game in your own classroom

What do you think the word responsible means?

Why do you think it is important to develop our ability to be responsible?

Think of something that you are completely responsible for. This means doing it without any help from anyone else.

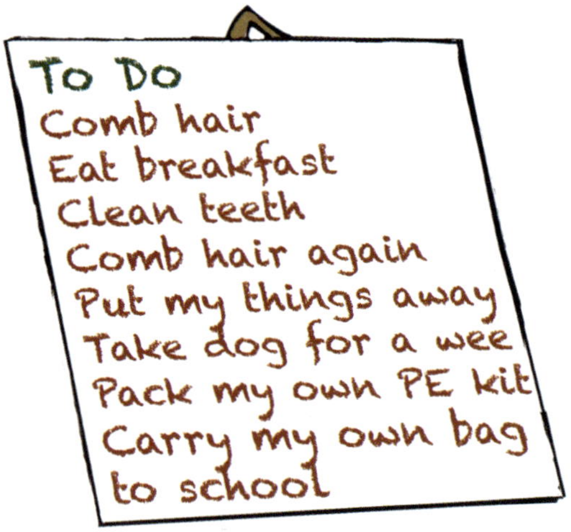

Think of something you are jointly responsible for. This means doing it with help from a friend or work partner.

Listing my responsibilities

In the table below, make a list of all those things you take responsibility for ***now*** in your classroom, you ***could*** take responsibility for in your classroom and which things you could ***share*** responsibility for with your partner or learning team.

What I take responsibility for **now**	What I take **joint** responsibility for now	What I could take responsibility for **next**
Eg. Having a pen to write with	Keeping my table tidy	Always put the top back on the white board marker

Think about the statements below. If you think you are responsible put an 'L' in the box, if you think your teacher is responsible put a 'T' in the box and if you think you share responsibility put an 'S':

If I am to be a successful learner I need to be able to talk about:	**(L)Learner, (T)Teacher, (S)Shared**
What I am learning and why I am learning it	
My goals and targets	
Where I am now, where I need to go and how I am going to get there	
What a high quality piece of work looks like	
How I am challenging myself	
How I will know when I have been successful	
What my strengths and weaknesses are	
What I need to do next and what I could achieve	
What I can do myself when I am faced with a problem	
How my work will be judged	
How to make improvements	
How to review my learning and the progress I have made	
Feeling proud of my real achievements	

The balance of responsibility

When we are able to see a problem we are well on the way to solving it.
"The problem with problems is, that I can never see what the problem is!"
Some people never see the problem, for some people they can see the problem but they don't do anything about it.

Look at the list of reasons why we don't solve problems and give an example of when you have not solved the problems because of that reason:

What was the problem?	**Why did you ignore it?**
	I didn't think it was my problem
	I saw it but ignored it
	I just couldn't be bothered
	It looked too hard
	I had no one to help me with it
	I didn't see the point of doing it
	Someone had told me I wouldn't be able to do it
	Somebody solved the problem for me

Choose one of the problems you have listed and think about how you could solve it.

Why is solving your own problems good for you?

Every time we see a problem and choose to do something about it (solve it ourselves with a partner or group) we make some Diamond Power. This helps our brain get even better at solving problems.

The more problems we solve the better we get at it! Just look at the number of branches in the brain of someone that solves lots of problems compared to someone that chooses not to.

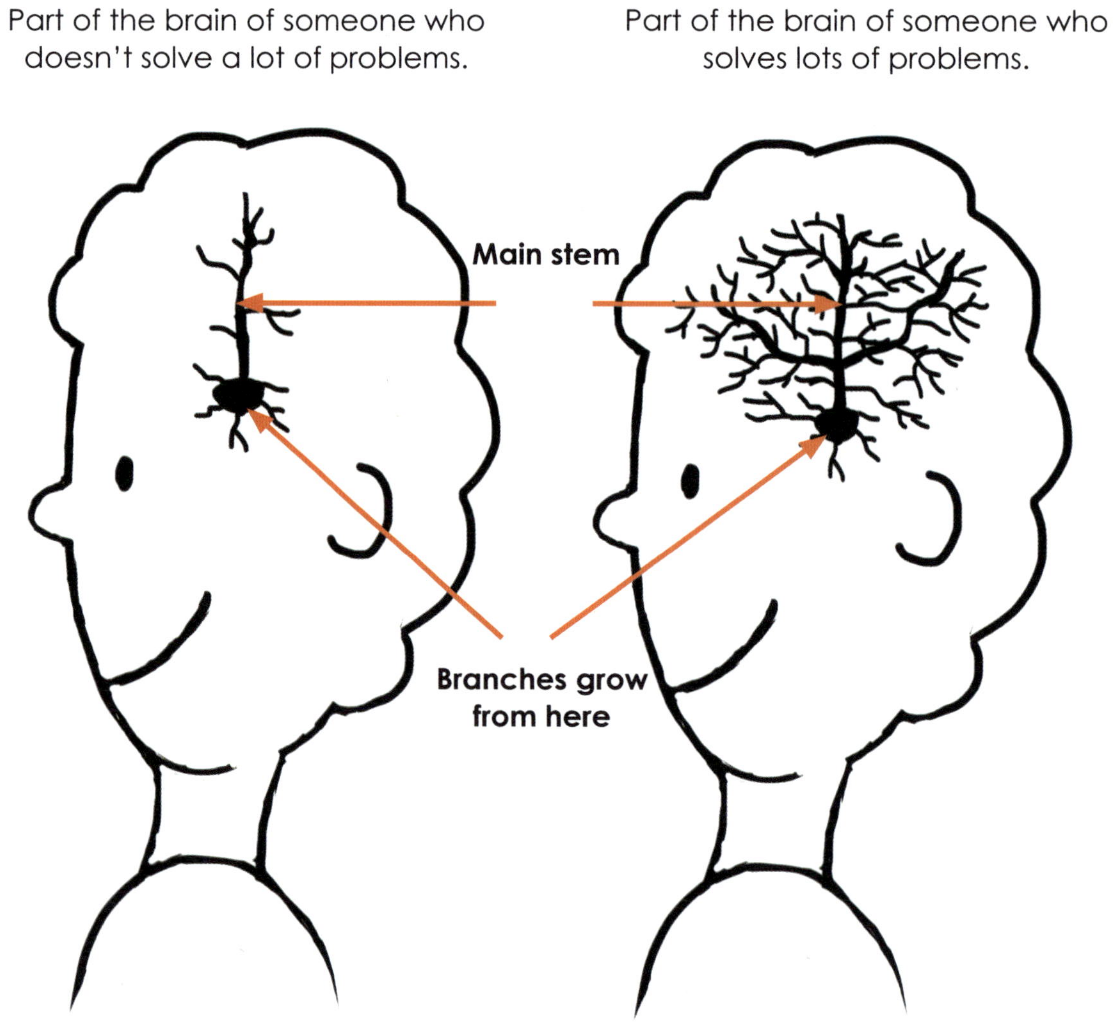

Which one are you?

Describe a problem you have solved

Draw a mind map of how you did it. Ask your teacher for help.

Playing the Diamond Power game with your class and teacher

Your teachers are so full of Diamond Power because they are always helping you. If you compare how much Diamond Power they have, compared to you, they are like a glass jar full of diamonds and you are probably only a quarter of the way up.

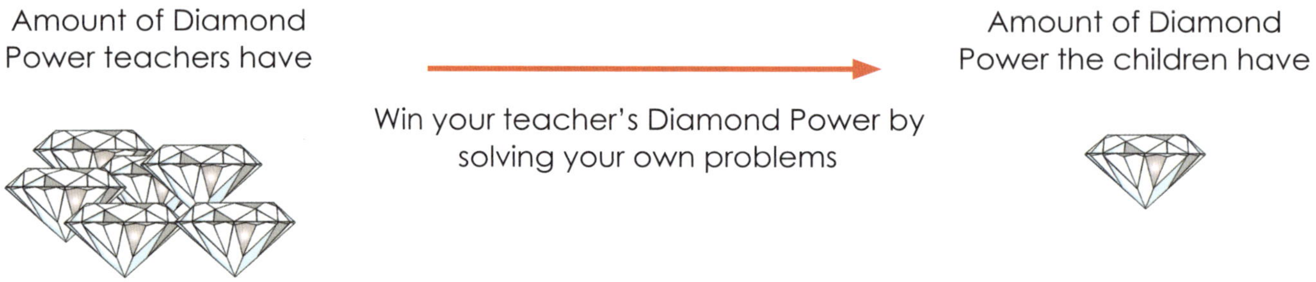

How to get Diamond Power from your teacher:

- Fill a glass jar full of plastic diamonds. This belongs to the teacher who has lots of Diamond Power. Have an empty jar next to the full one. This represents the fact the class has very little Diamond Power.
- Agree on the problems to be solved so you can develop your Diamond Power.
- Display them on a class Diamond Charter somewhere in the classroom.
- If your teacher has to help anyone solve the agreed problems that week, he/she keeps his/her diamonds and the class doesn't win them.
- If all the class manage to solve the problems without help from the teacher, the teacher must hand over one of their diamonds to the class. (Even being reminded about what to do by the teacher means the teacher keeps his/ her diamonds).
- The game is to win as many diamonds as you can in one term.
- You can have a competition between the other classes and see which class wins the most Diamond Power.

Part Five

Become a Better Learner

So what now?

In this section you will:

- Be asked to think about what you have read, understood and learned (this is called reflective thinking)
- Be introduced to a way of planning what you will do with this new learning, to help you become a more successful learner.

You have now thought about: talking about learning, how you see yourself as a learner, your goals and dreams, 'bouncebackability', how you feel when you are learning, challenging yourself, being a team player, making choices and taking responsibility.

So you have been thinking like a learner!

What do you do now? It is very important that you do something with your new knowledge and understanding. This is not just a book to read but a guide to enable you to think more deeply about your learning and then take action so that you become an even better learner! The only person who can improve the learning is the learner and that means YOU!!

What has most interested you in thinking like a learner?

What have you learned about yourself?

How do you now see yourself as a learner?

Becoming a better learner - thinking about improvement

What do think are your learning strengths?

How much effort do you make in your learning?

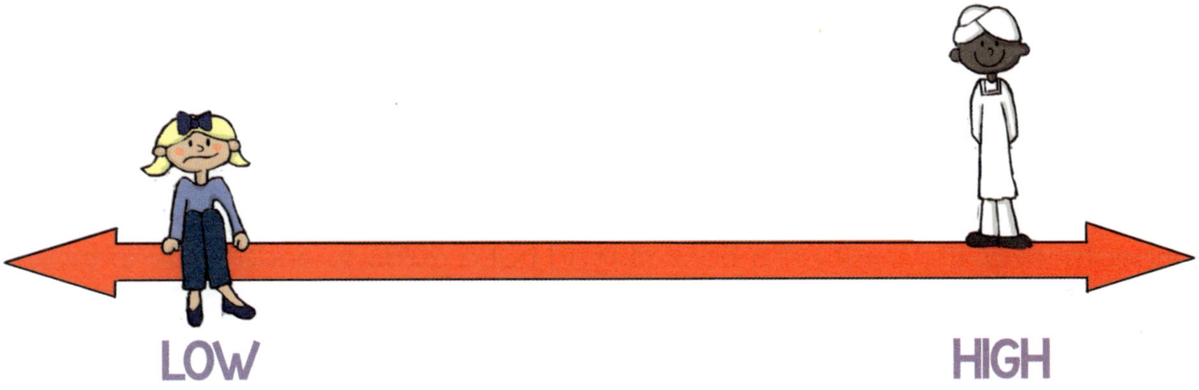

Mark on the line where you think your effort level is most of the time – be really honest! Put the date against the mark you make.

How much effort are you prepared to make? Return to this in about 2 weeks – where will you aim to put your mark then?

What do you want to improve? Why is this important to you?

What do you think you need to do next?

How will you know if you have made progress?

We have really enjoyed writing this book and thinking about all the wonderful learners that we work with! We really hope that you have found this book useful – we hope that you have learned about yourself as a learner and that you now know a little more about how to become the very best you can be!

In Part Six you will find some more information and other ways to record your thinking about your learning – you could even keep a learning journal to record how you are becoming an even better learner!

Remember to celebrate... it is important to feel proud of your achievements if you have worked really hard for them.

Remember that it is up to you to make the difference and that everyone can make improvements.

Good luck in the next section!

Part Six

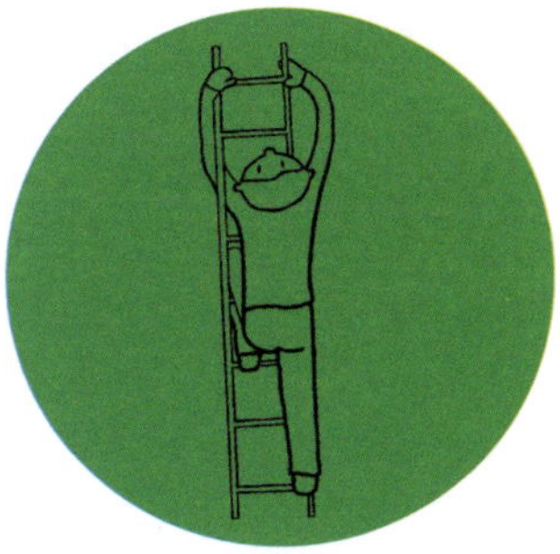

Thinking and Learning in Action

Thinking and Learning in Action!

How do I get more gem power?

- Look at the next few pages and decide which gem power you are interested in getting better at.
- Once you have decided, start from the bottom of the ladder.
- As you move up the ladder think about what you do to prove you are on the step you think you are on.
- Finally, think about what you need to do next to get up to the next step on the ladder.
- Practice so you can move up even further.

Where am I on the team work ladder?

The Amethyst Power is learning with a partner and the Topaz Power is working with a team of three or more. Have a look on the ladder below and see where you think you might be. Give examples of what you have done to reach that high on the ladder.

Amethyst and Topaz Power	Examples of what I have done to reach this part of the ladder
I am a brilliant member of a team and can tell others what to do to be a good team member	
I select when to work alone or with others	
I respect and work with other people's views and ideas	
I know what the rules of good team work are and can follow them when working in a team	
I know all of the team work rules	
I can share ideas on what has to be learned when working with another person	
I understand what is going on even when working in a team of two or more	
I work alongside another person and share by listening and talking	
I learn by doing what the other person did	
I find it really tough to work with others	

Start here and work your way up

Climbing the Ruby Power Ladder

The way you treat others when you learn will slow down your learning and theirs, or help you and them, grow your learning.
Ruby Power is what you make every time you choose to think of something positive about another person. If you turn those positive thoughts into positive words you make even more and if you turn the words into positive action you make even more.

On this Ruby Power development ladder where do you think you are? Give examples of what you have done to reach that high on the ladder.

Ruby Power	**Examples of what I have done to reach this part of the ladder**
I get lots of pleasure out of learning and supporting others in many different situations	
I feel really good when I do some act of random kindness for no reason	
I understand how others might feel when they make a mistake, are disappointed or sad	
I notice when someone might need some help and offer to help them	
I listen to others when they talk, with eyes and ears; it makes the listener feel valued	
I praise others for their success by smiling at them and telling them **why** what they did was good	
I praise others for their success by smiling at them and telling them **what** they did was good	
I smile a lot and make others feel good	
I accept encouragement and praise from others	
I do not like giving or receiving praise	Start here and work your way up

Am I a Diamond Power Climber?

Where am I on the problem solving (Diamond Power) ladder? Have a look on the ladder below and see where you think you might be. Give examples of what you have done to reach that high on the ladder.

Diamond Power	Examples of what I have done to reach this part of the ladder
I get a real buzz from solving problems. I look for them everywhere and try to solve them	
When facing a problem I help others see their responsibility in solving it	
When faced with a problem, I take responsibility for solving it	
When faced with a problem I decide if it's best to work alone or in a team	
When faced with problems; I solve them by myself if possible, if it is too tough I talk to friends about it	
I see the problem and will try and solve it sometimes	
I see the problem and need encouragement from the teacher to solve it	
I see the problem and with some help can ask questions about it	
I see the problem but like to be told what to do, when and how	
It's never my problem it is always someone else's	

Start here and work your way up

Can I stay calm and focused?

Where am I on the keeping focused (Sapphire Power) and 'bouncebackability' (Emerald Power) ladder? Have a look on the ladder below and see where you think you might be. Give examples of what you have done to reach that high on the ladder.

Sapphire and Emerald Power	**Examples of what I have done to reach this part of the ladder**
I loves challenges and understand why mistakes are important and I keep the monster in the brain under control	
Even with the biggest monster distraction, I keep focused until I've completed what I have to do	
I can recognise the monster distractions and control them so I can keep focused	
Even when provoked by others, or making mistakes or being disappointed, I can remain calm. I try to tame the monster in the brain	
I can get really excited or very disappointed and still bounce back to the task	
I am aware of the monster distractions when reminded	
I try tricky things and when a mistake is made, remain calm and start again even if lots of mistakes are made	
I don't mind taking a risk in learning even though I might get it wrong. When a mistake is made, I remain calm	
I find it difficult to control my excitement, disappointment, fear of making mistakes. The monster in my brain is more in control	
I stick at some tasks for short periods; the monster distraction sometimes wins!	

Start here and work your way up

Gem Power facts

Things you might want to know about the chemicals that each gem power represents:

Ruby Power:

One of the things that helps you make more oxytocin is by supporting each other; **pointing out each other's success** and letting someone know when they are doing well.

When you make **oxytocin** it helps you work together better as a team. It helps you remember and understand what people say and do, especially if people in the team are **smiling and happy.**

Oxytocin helps you develop trust in the team and it gives you the ability to take risks in your learning.

When you **smile, laugh or relax** for a short while you make **serotonin.** This gives you a sense of well being, reduced stress and makes you feel good.

When you **laugh a lot** you make **endorphin.** This is your happy chemical and makes you feel really good.

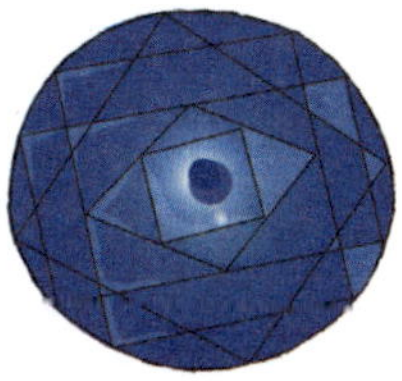

Sapphire Power:

When you move some of your muscles you make a chemical called dopamine. Dopamine makes you feel good, stimulates movement and dulls pain. It also helps you keep focused to fight off the monster distraction.

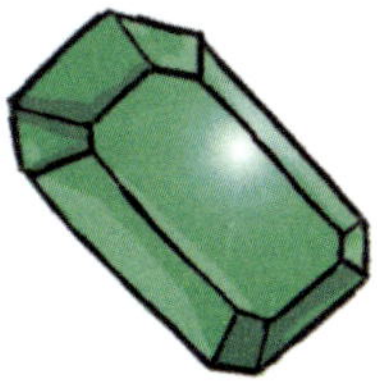

Emerald Power:

When you **run, move or you are challenged** a lot you make **adrenaline.** This **energises your body** and sends food and oxygen all over your body to make it work better. This helps you think better and make better memories. When you are challenged and you feel 'butterflies' in your tummy, it's the Emerald Power that makes you feel like that. Once you get used to that feeling you can learn to control it rather than the Emerald Power controlling you!

When you are **stressed** you make lots of **adrenaline and cortisol** which **switches off your thinking** and too much can damage your brain. This is when you lose control of your Emerald Power.

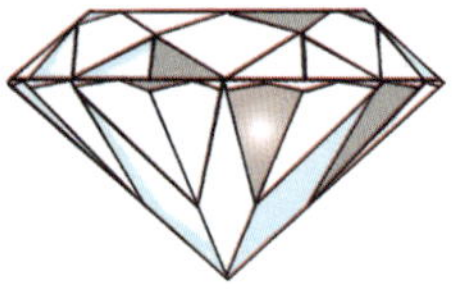

Diamond Power:

The brain is made up of about 100 billion brain cells called neurones. A million is quite a lot! 1,000,000. A billion is a thousand million, 1,000,000,000, so a hundred billion is 100,000,000,000! That's quite a lot of neurones.

Each neurone is made up of little branches that stick out of it called dendrites. As we learn something new, another dendrite grows.

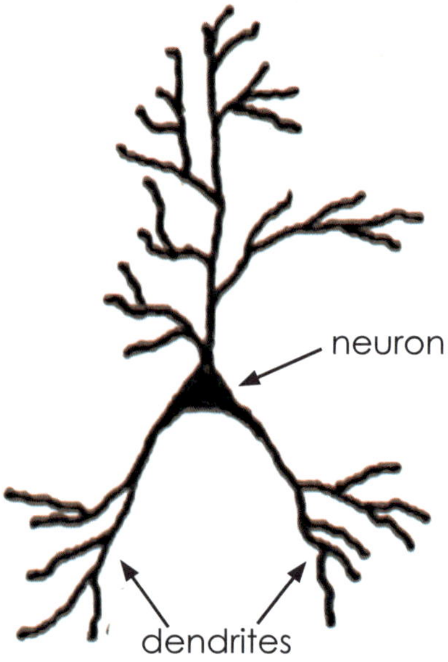

Learning = dendrite growth

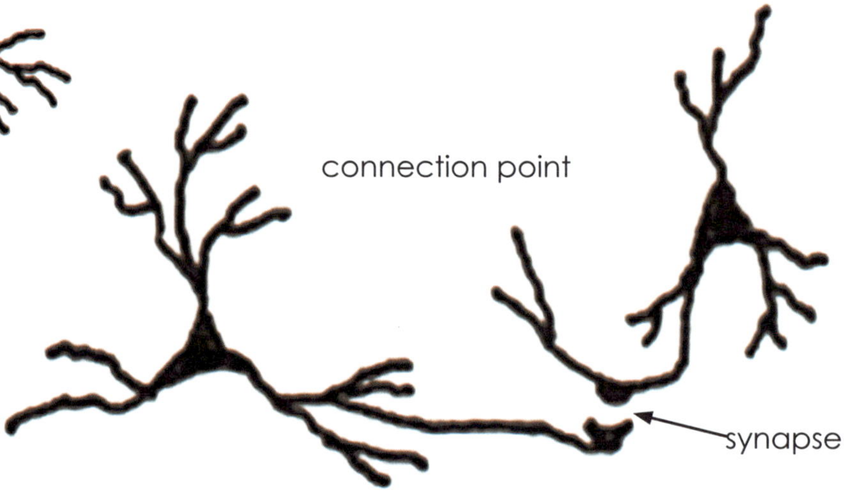

It takes some time for dendrites to grow, that's why it seems to take ages to learn something. When two dendrites grow and come close together there is a little gap between them; **this is how messages are sent from one brain cell to another** helping us use what we have learned.

The more we practice doing something, the thicker the dendrites become, the faster the signal travels and the easier it becomes to use what we have learned.

If we practice lots, the connection between the dendrites becomes a double connection and we can remember and use what we have learned for a long time. If we do the same thing again and again it then becomes a habit; something we do without even thinking about it! If you listen or watch something that you want to learn, you grow dendrites for learning what you are listening to or watching.

Your Diamond Power is your ability to solve problems and learn! The more problems you solve the better you get at learning.

You are naturally sparkly like a diamond because your dendrites grow, like your lungs know how to breathe in air. If you want even more Diamond Power you need to work at it though. No one else can grow your dendrites for you!

Independent Research Plan	
Name:	Class/Year group:
Project/topic focus:	
Why have you chosen this project/topic?	
What will your end result/final product be?	
What resources will you need?	
How much time will you need?	
How would you like your learning to be reviewed?	
Signed:	Date:
Teacher Response:	
Signed:	Date:

My Learning Tools

Individual Planning Sheet	
Name:	
Date:	
Area of learning:	
What do you want to learn/ find out?	
What do you need? (e.g. visit library, use ICT, work with someone else etc)	
How long will you need?	
What will your result look like?	
How will you know if you have been successful?	

My Learning Tools

Learning Log	
Name:	
Date:	
Area of learning:	
What were you doing? (E.g. working on your own, with a partner, in a group, with the teacher).	
What have you learned?	
How will this learning help you?	
What would you like to learn next?	

Thoughts, Questions, Plans and Actions...

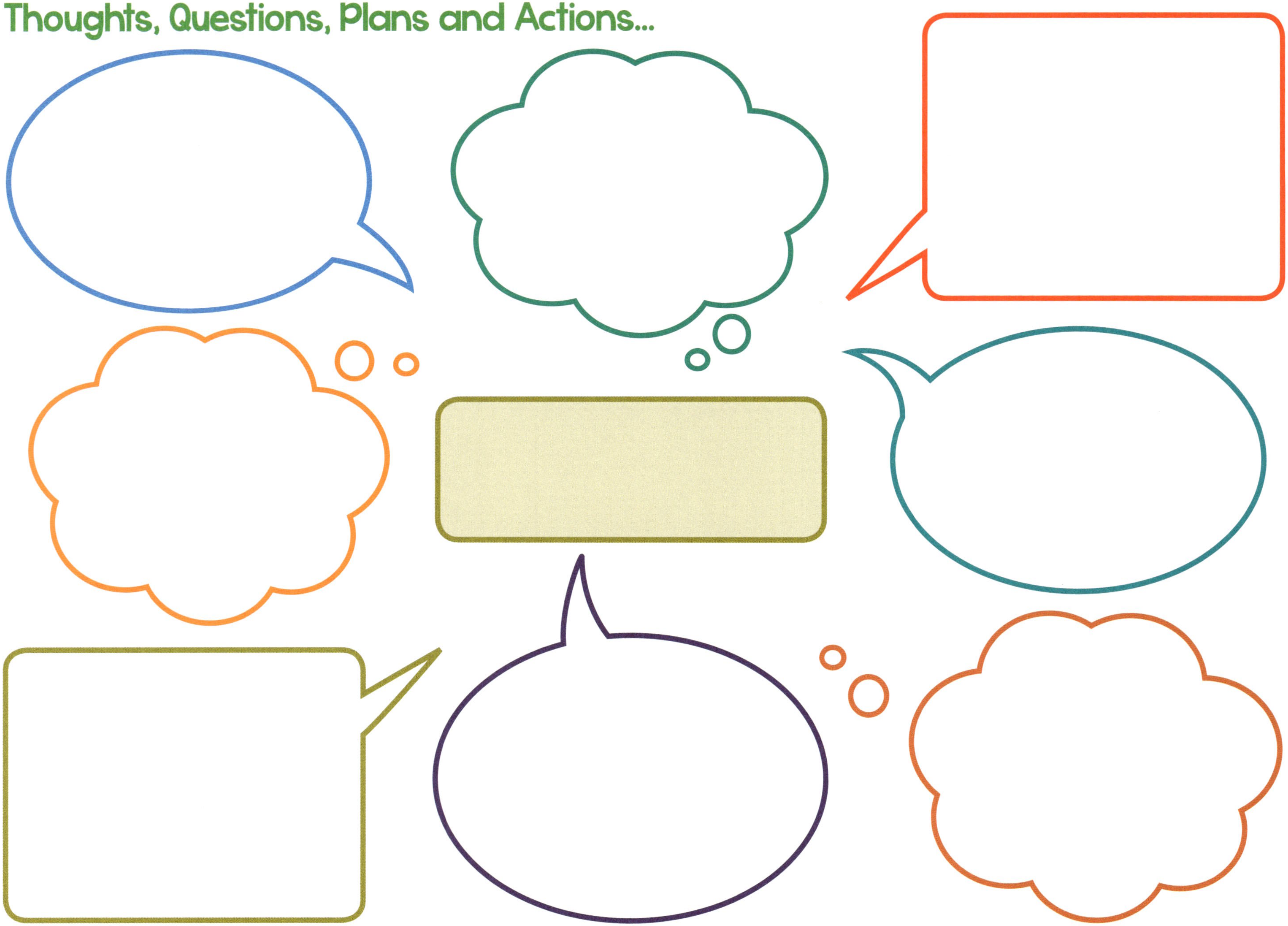

Am I a Successful Learner?

If you...	What will it look like?	What will it sound like?
Are ready for learning		
Are a good listener		
Concentrate		
Work well in a team		
Persevere		

Am I a Successful Learner?

If you...	What will it look like?	What will it sound like?
Work hard to solve problems		
Co-operate		
Help other learners		
Can work independently		
Enjoy your learning		

Am I a Successful Learner?

If you...	What will it look like?	What will it sound like?

My Presentation Plan

Work with your parents or teacher to draw up a plan of action to research your favourite topic for a presentation to class, using the skills you have learned in this book.